Financial Freedom

Understanding Money Management

Brian S. Hankerson, CPA

Unless otherwise indicated, all Scripture quotations are taken from the King James Version of the Bible.

Financial Freedom: Understanding Money Management
(formerly titled *Seven Biblical Principles for Money Management*)

ISBN-10 0-98323081-1
ISBN-13 978-0-98323081-6

Copyright © 2011 Global Financial Ministries Inc.
globalministriesint.org

Published by Global Financial Ministries Inc.

Editorial by Jordan Media Services
Fort Worth, TX | www.jordanmediaservices.com

Cover design and typesetting by Ken Fraser Designs
kenfraser@charter.net

Printed in the United States of America

Dedication

This book is dedicated to my wonderful grand-daughter, Jordan Amarie McLemore. Jordan, you are such a blessing to me. You have been my motivation to complete this project. Though I started years ago, it was not until God blessed us with you that I really became inspired to complete this book. God's Word directs me to leave an inheritance to my children's children. The blessings that will flow from this book will allow me to begin responding to that mandate.

Thank You

Acknowledgements

A world of thanks…..

To my wife, Tina, thanks for all your support and encouragement, and your enduring love and friendship. You are a wonderful wife and an awesome mother to our children. I love you dearly.

To my children, you are the best children a parent could ever hope or pray for. I am extremely proud of each of you. I look forward to your great successes in life. Remember, always keep God first.

To my parents, it's actually hard to put into words how much I appreciate you. You have been great parents, and friends. I thank God for you and pray that He continues to richly bless you.

To Bishop Henry and Pastor Carol Fernandez, thank you for your guidance and encouragement. Bishop, I value your wisdom and appreciate your spiritual guidance. You are both great leaders and I am so blessed to have the opportunity to support the vision God has given you.

TABLE OF CONTENTS

INTRODUCTION

In this day and age of a ever-changing and unpredictable economy, there is one area that continues to be essential to our day-to-day existence: MONEY! Throughout history, money has been a common and consistent element in society. The need, the desire, and the benefits of possessing money have remained the same throughout the world.

Money has been defined as "a commodity of value, the primary means by which we acquire the essentials of life as well as items of luxury." Money existed in Biblical days and served essentially the same purpose it does today.

As believers in Christ Jesus and the Word of God, we must realize that money, though created and controlled by man, actually belongs to God. Like many other things on this earth, money has been entrusted to us as stewards. It is not evil, as many might believe: it's actually essential in today's society. The Bible states in Ecclesiastes 10:19 that money "answerth all things." Therefore, it is of extreme importance that we better understand the intricacies of money: how to earn it, how to keep it, how to grow it and how to spend it, all according to God's Word. We *must* learn to be better stewards of God's money.

Remember, God wants us to prosper financially, but we must first learn to be good stewards with what He has entrusted to us. This requires employing the biblical principles provided in the Word of God regarding money management. It is then that we will show ourselves faithful and be prepared and positioned to receive the supernatural blessing God has promised.

Some of the key biblical principles we, as Christians, must begin to apply to our lives to become stewards are as follows:

- Institute a comprehensive financial plan.
- Assess our current financial status.
- Eliminate current debt.
- Avoid new debt.
- Tithe 10% or more.
- Give to charities or the needy.
- Create long and short-term savings (20%).
- Invest savings to create growth and income.
- Analyze your insurance for proper coverage.
- Prepare an estate plan to avoid death taxes.
- Eliminate wasted spending.
- Seek new sources of producing income.
- Prepare for retirement (self-funded).
- Implement a succession plan for your children.
- Reduce excessive income taxes.
- Create a cash surplus.
- Make wise, informed business decisions.
- Seek the advice of experts.
- Be patient.

In this book I will present some of the key biblical principles for successful money management contained in the Word of God. I will also attempt to impart additional information that I feel is critical to achieving financial prosperity.

FORWARD

There is one area that continues to cause many Christians to experience tremendous stress and discomfort. It is the area of finances and money management. Many well-meaning Christians show great zeal in the areas of prayer, praise and worship. However, when it comes to their finances, they are struggling mightily. They are bound by a spirit of poverty and are not prospering as the Lord has promised in His Word. This spirit of poverty has gotten a stronghold on many in the body of Christ for the specific purpose of causing them to become ineffective for the Kingdom of God. It's very hard to be effective for the Kingdom when worrying about how essential and critical bills and obligations will be paid from one month to the next.

God does not desire for you to live like that. He desires for you to prosper (3 John 1:2), and He has given you the power to get wealth (Deuteronomy 8:18). This is the year of overflow, and many will experience this overflow in their finances. However, before you can experience this overflow, you must properly position yourself to receive. As it relates to the area of finances, that means you must become good stewards of God's resources. You must be faithful with little things or a few things so that He might reward you with mighty things. You must educate yourself to be able to properly handle the blessings that will come your way as promised in God's Word.

This book sets forth seven key principles that must be applied to your life. When applied, you are being obedient to what God's Word says about being a good steward. Also, you are adhering to sound economic principles that have been proven to work throughout history.

Take these principles and memorize them so that the application is automatic in every financial decision you make. Remember, this is the year of overflow and God desires that you prosper as your soul prospers. Be Blessed.

Bishop Henry Fernandez
The Faith Center Ministries, Inc.

Chapter I

Breaking the Spirit of Poverty

God has a financial system already in place and the Bible outlines how to properly navigate this system with success. The Bible has much to say about how to use money in day-to-day activity. In fact, in 16 of 38 parables in the New Testament Jesus addressed how to handle money and possessions. The Scriptures reveal that God doesn't have a problem with Christians having money. Actually, God's financial plan for the believer is well above the average Christian's expectations. Christians have been programmed with a poverty mentality and a spirit of poverty that is not from God's Word.

According to *Deuteronomy 8:18*, God has given each believer the power to get wealth so that He might establish His covenant in the earth. This is part of our economic destiny. God has placed within every individual the ability to take control of their personal finances, to live successfully and to make a positive contribution on society. However, before most become young adults they have already been programmed by a system that keeps them from reaching their full economic destiny. That poverty-mentality system will control most of them and cause them to spend the rest of their lives in financial bondage.

God wants people who can be trusted with money. He wants us to get our houses in order, not just so our needs can be met but so we will be able to reach out and help those around us. This will put us in position to show the love of Christ through our actions and not just with words, so that His covenant might be established on earth.

In today's time of an unpredictable economy, many have become paralyzed by fear of the unknown. Some reports indicate that inflation is at a notable low and interest rates are at an attractive rate. Yet, other reports indicate that unemployment is at an all-time high. The stock market experiences unprecedented swings from losses to gains. Even with this uncertainty, there are many who continue to prosper while a great portion of society continue to live in lack. The rich seem to be getting richer, while the poor are getting poorer. This is not a perception, but a fact.

The rich are getting richer because they are employing **sound economic principles** that insure that wealth is constantly accumulated and economic independence is maintained in spite of the state of the economy. These economic principles are time-tested and proven to work for everyone who employs those principles. They work in times of economic growth or recession. The poor, on the other hand, are getting poorer because they are constantly applying economic principles that contribute to economic dependency. They look more towards quick fixes than long-term solutions. Although good sound economic principles are simple and straightforward, most people are not willing to make the commitment or take the time and effort to learn the principles of financial success and then have the discipline to apply them in their lives.

Economics is stewardship. It is the study of how people make decisions regarding money: managing, investing and creating wealth. Clearly, the best type of economy is capitalism (the free enterprise system), where each individual has the right and responsibility to produce, save, invest and create wealth.

The Bible teaches that God created man, the universe, the heavens and the earth. God operates in the spirit and in the natural.... Man was created in God's image and given dominion over His creation. God taught man the basic principles of economics so he could become a good steward over the wealth God had provided. As a result, God mandated in His Word that there would be a reward for good stewardship and a price to pay for being a bad steward.

The sound principles of money management being applied by many wealthy individuals today are consistent with God's principles of **stewardship** set forth in the Bible. They are not complex, unreasonable or burdensome. They are simple and effective. As Christians, we must diligently seek this knowledge and consistently apply it to our lives.

It never ceases to amaze me that throughout this country, most Christians find themselves in economic despair. If a survey were taken in churches across America today and the question asked, "Who is in need of a financial blessing?" no doubt most would respond in the affirmative. Yet these are God's children—people who are faithfully seeking to please God and do His will. These are individuals who are saved, sanctified and filled with the Holy Ghost. They study the Word and pray, yet they are still experiencing consistent economic despair and lack. They are bound by a spirit of poverty.

The spirit of poverty is so well entrenched in the house of God that we are often blinded to the direction and instruction contained in the very Word of God that will guarantee our financial success. This spirit of poverty is not of God but of the enemy. Money is a powerful tool in the hands of faithful Christians. Because of the impact this revelation can have for the kingdom of God, and the powerful blow it can deliver to the kingdom of darkness, Satan has gone to great lengths to keep the Church confused regarding the role of money in the hands of believers.

Myths and certain religious traditions have been very successful in keeping us confused regarding money. We have been programmed to have the wrong attitude about money. These myths take on many forms and span different cultural and economic backgrounds. Some of these myths include:

- Money is the root of all evil.

- Poverty is a sign of spirituality. Christians are supposed to be poor to show their spirituality.

- It is easier for a camel to go through the eye of a needle than for a rich man to go to heaven. Therefore, you can't have treasures on earth and expect to go to heaven.

- Since money is part of the world's system, and you are supposed to be heavenly-minded, you should not talk about money in church.

- All preachers want is your money; they're not concerned about your soul.

- Jesus told the rich young ruler to sell his

possessions and give his money away; therefore, if you love Jesus, you aren't supposed to
have riches on earth.

• If you really trust Jesus and use faith, He will
meet all your financial needs without you having to do anything about your circumstances.

There are many other distorted biblical principles,
all based on misinformation. Even though none of
them are true, they impact the very hearts and souls
of many Christians and non-Christians alike. These
beliefs are responsible for robbing the believer of their
economic inheritance. There are many other Scriptures
that prove these myths to be untrue and show us that
God wants us to prosper economically. We must seek
out this knowledge contained in the Word and change
the course of our lives. Hosea 4:6, states, *"My people are
destroyed for lack of knowledge"*.

The Bible not only tells us that God wants us to
prosper, but it also indicates that there is a purpose for
our economic success. He wants us to plan our financial
decisions. He wants us to invest and seek high returns,
to save, to give, to avoid debt, to pay our fair share of
taxes, to stay abreast of current trends and developments, to seek knowledge, to work and be productive,
to be good stewards, to be honest in our dealings, to be
prudent and not wasteful, and to pass on this knowledge. These are spiritually-based principles of money
management that also happen to be sound economic
principles that create wealth and financial success.

The Bible points out that there is a close correlation
between skillful money management and spiritual
things. Jesus Himself told the parable that the reward

for good stewardship includes a spiritual reward upon His return.

Some of the more pertinent scriptural references relating to financial success are listed in Appendix I. There are many more scriptures that can be explored on this subject. Remember, God wants us to prosper financially as our soul prospers.

Chapter 2

PRINCIPLE #1
Know Your Current Financial State Of Affairs

B efore you can improve your current financial status, you must first determine your current financial status. Most people are not aware of where they are financially. Typically, they believe they are in pretty good financial condition. It's not until they carefully and thoroughly examine their financial condition, including looking at long term and short term goals, that they can have a clear picture of their true financial condition. For others, one look at their bank account, wallet or purse, and it is clear their financial status is not good. In fact, it's usually pretty bad.

Your financial status involves more than determining how much of your paycheck remains at the end of the month. You must determine where the money went and how it was spent. Then, you are in a position to analyze your financial status.

Another step in determining your financial status is to determine your net worth. And finally, determining your financial status must involve an analysis of your progress towards reaching certain financial goals such as retirement, funding your children's college fund, owning your dream home, taking a trip around the world, or starting a business. All of these things must be taken into account when trying to get an accurate assessment of your financial health.

Have you ever experienced receiving your check on Friday and by Monday it was all gone? You wonder where it went and how you will make it until the next pay day. Well, you are not alone. The majority of America lives from paycheck to paycheck. Have you ever wondered what would happen if you were to lose your job and were not able to find work for a few months? Would you face losing your home or car? Could you still support your family? These are indeed eye-opening questions. By living from paycheck to paycheck, you obviously are not saving any money for such a time as this. By living from paycheck to paycheck, you end up paying many bills late and incurring late charges that you can't afford. You are actually making matters worse. You work hard all week and pay your money to someone who had nothing to do with the earning of it, and your circumstances are getting worse instead of better. Everyone is getting paid except you, the one who actually earned the money. Something is very wrong with this picture.

The money we earn actually belongs to God. We are merely stewards over that money. The Word of God teaches us that everything belongs to God. That includes money and financial resources. He made us stewards over everything on the earth and He gave us a command to be "good stewards." His Word also states that there is a reward to being a good steward. As you analyze your current financial status, you must ask yourself, "Am I being a good steward of God's resources?" These resources include our time, talents and, of course, our money.

Moreover it is required in stewards, that a man be found faithful. **1 Corinthian 4:2**

For every beast of the forest is mine, and the cattle upon a thousand hills. I know all the fowls of the mountains: and the wild beasts of the field are mine. **Psalm 50:10-12**

And so he that had received five talents came and brought other five talents, saying, Lord, thou deliveredst unto me five talents: behold, I have gained beside them five talents more.

His lord said unto him, Well done, thou good and faithful servant: thou hast been faithful over a few things, I will make thee ruler over many things: enter thou into the joy of thy lord. **Matthew 25:20**

Since there are both spiritual and natural rewards for being a good steward, you should be motivated to strive toward being the best steward possible. There are many examples to prove that when you properly manage your resources, you better position yourself for success. The Word of God teaches us that if we are faithful over a few things, God will make us ruler over many things. As a matter of fact, the Bible teaches us that God desires for us to prosper in all aspects of life including our finances.

STEP 1 – ANALYZE CASH FLOW

To properly analyze your cash flow, you must examine your spending habits. Since spending habits may vary from week to week, this examination should take place over several months. I recommend three months. To do this, you should record every penny you spend. Utilize your checkbook or debit card as much as possible. This will at least create a record of what was spent and the purpose for which it was spent. Next, always get a receipt whenever you spend cash. That includes paying for tolls, gas and parking. I have found it helpful to keep a folder or envelop in my car to hold these receipts.

At the end of each month all expenses should be summarized by category, either in the computer using accounting software such as Quicken or a spreadsheet program such as Excel. Listed below are some of the categories to use in summarizing your expenses:

- Housing (Mortgage or rent, maintenance, etc.)
- Clothing
- Automobile (Loan Payments)
- Child-related expenses
- Gas and repairs
- Utilities
- Insurance – Auto
- Phone (Home and Cell)
- Insurance – Medical
- Food – Lunch
- Insurance – Life
- Work related expenses
- Insurance – Other
- Medical
- Food – Grocery
- Sundry Items

- Entertainment
- Transportation (Tolls/Parking)
- Church
- Other Charities
- Income Taxes

Once you have summarized at least three months of expenses, they should be averaged. Congratulations, you now have a report that will show you just how you are spending your hard-earned money. Using a calculator, you can compute the relative percentages of each expense category in comparison to total expenses. This will become more meaningful when you develop your budget in Chapter 4.

To many of us, this summary on how we are spending our money can be an eye opening experience. It has been said that if you want to know something about a person's life look at how they spend their money. This analysis will show the truth about your spending and living habits. It will indicate what your priorities are and what matters to you. What does yours say about you?

STEP 2 – DETERMINE NET WORTH

Another component of determining your current financial status is to measure your net worth. Everyone has a net worth: both businesses and individuals. Net worth is defined as the difference between your net assets and your net liabilities. Another way to state it is the difference between what you own and what you owe. If you own assets worth $40,000 and you owe

$25,000 in debt, then your net worth is $15,000.

In computing your net worth, you should list all of your assets separate from your liabilities. To properly complete this schedule you will need to do an inventory of everything you own. Count it even if you owe money on it. That includes your house. After the inventory has been taken and everything listed, you must next estimate the current value of each item. One way to estimate the value of an item is to consider the amount you could receive for it if you were to sell it in an arms-length transaction. Also, the price must be one that will cause the item to be sold in a reasonable amount of time (not too soon and not too long).

Next, you must determine your liabilities, or debts. You should always know what you owe others. If one of your goals is to get out of debt, you must first know just what you owe. If you don't know, contact your creditors to find out what balances you do owe. Ask for the current payoff amount.

Another way to determine what you owe is to get a copy of your credit report from one or each of the three major credit-reporting agencies (Equifax, Experian and Trans-Union). This can be helpful because there may be old debts you owe that you have forgotten about or debt that you may desire to dispute for whatever reason.

After you have assessed how you spend your money on a monthly basis, and what your current net worth is, then it is time to examine how well you are doing toward reaching your dreams, goals and desires.

STEP 3 – ASSESS YOUR PROGRESS

The final component in determining your current financial status is to determine the progress you have made toward reaching your long term financial goals, dreams and desires. For example, if it is your goal to retire at the age of 50 and receive $60,000 annually for the rest of your life, it becomes very important to have a plan in place and to be working that plan for your desired outcome. If you are 40 years old and have invested only $40,000 in an Individual Retirement Account (IRA) or other retirement instrument such as a 401(K) plan, you're actually not doing too well. Computations show that to meet this goal you will need to accumulate $750,000 by the time you retire at age 50. Well, you are 40 and you have only $40,000. Once again, you're not doing too well toward meeting the desired goal. Something has to change.

To determine how you are doing toward meeting your goals, the following process must be followed for each item:

1. Identify long term goals that are important to you and your family.

2. Determine when you want to achieve a particular goal.

3. Determine the amount of money you will need to achieve the goal.

4. Measure the amount of money you have accumulated and set aside towards meeting the financial requirement for that goal.

5. When you compare the amounts in Steps 3 and 4, you will derive the difference or the shortfall. This represents the amount you will

need to accumulate before the date determined in Step 2.

6. Now you know what you need and the
amount of time you have to accumulate it.

7. Make adjustments to your budgeted spending to enable you to start saving towards your
established goals.

8. Secure the money in a savings or investment plan to insure that it will be there when
needed.

Let's walk through an example of the above steps.
Assume the following facts.

You are 40 years old and you plan to send
your child to college when she graduates from
high school. She is currently in the seventh
grade. You therefore have five full years before
you will need the funds. The school she plans to
attend will cost $70,000 over a four-year period.
To date, you have accumulated $20,000 in a spe-
cial investment fund. Therefore, your shortfall
currently is $50,000. By dividing the shortfall by
the number of years left to meet the goal, we
will get $10,000. That means, on average, you
will need to accumulate $10,000 per year for
the next five years. Fortunately, due to the time
value of money and the growth rate you have
received from the investment fund you are in,
you will only need to invest $8,500 per year.

This type of analysis must be done for each item you
identify as your goal. Yes, it is a very time-consuming

and detailed process, but it is absolutely necessary to gain control of your finances. This is your first step to financial prosperity. It is very difficult to get where you want to go without knowing where you are. Once you know these three things, it becomes as simple as drawing a map or charting a course towards your desired outcome. Now, you are on your way to financial success, stability, economic independence and true prosperity.

Chapter 3

PRINCIPLE #2
Develop A Personal Financial Plan

*A prudent person foresees the danger ahead
and takes precautions; the simpleton goes blindly
on and suffers the consequences.*
Proverbs 22:3

Developing a personal financial plan is equivalent to developing a road map to chart a course for reaching your destination. To develop such a plan, you must first identify your goals. Identifying your short term, mid term and long term life and financial goals is the first and most important step towards meeting those goals. In the process of setting goals, you must understand who you are in God and what He desires and expects of you. You must also recognize and believe that God wants you to prosper in all aspects of life. He doesn't want you "just getting by." His desire is for you to prosper exceedingly. Remember, you are God's representative here on earth.

HOW TO SET GOALS

Now that you know how prosperous your life and that of your family is to be, you can began setting reasonable goals—goals that will please God. Since you are setting goals that may impact your life for years to come, you should exercise caution in identifying these goals. Recognize that because you are setting goals that are pleasing to God, you must seek His guidance and direction. This should not be taken lightly. As you chart the course for your life, you can expect that your life will begin to change dramatically. Remember, you have already determined that you are not currently meeting your goals. Actually, in some cases you may conclude that you have not set any meaningful goals.

God will direct you through this process. Remember, He said in His Word that those who seek Him will find Him. As you identify your goals, don't be afraid to think and dream big. Also, don't leave out the smaller things. By identifying your specific goals and putting together a written plan of action to achieve them, you now have a basis on which to measure your success and a way to hold yourself accountable. Writing your goals makes them more real and not just a dream or idle words. When you realize that your dreams can actually be achieved by implementing a well thought plan of action, you will become more motivated and focused on achieving them.

One of the primary stumbling blocks many encounter in reaching their goals lies in their own financial constraints. Most cannot envision how to fund their dreams and aspirations. But with proper planning and time, many goals and dreams can be met and exceeded.

Over many years of being in the financial consulting business, I have found the following list to be representative of one's goals, dreams and desires:

- Fund a child's education
- Own a vacation home

- Travel throughout the world
- Endow your favorite charity
- Start a business venture
- Secure retirement
- Obtain financial independence
- Own a dream home
- Become debt free
- Go to school
- Retire early
- Buy a car
- Set up a trust fund for grandchildren
- Own real estate throughout the country

Well, to achieve these goals you must plan for them and work toward reaching them by insuring that you have the financial ability to reach them.

When setting goals you must try to be very specific in identifying the goal and the related cost of achieving the goal. For example, if you want to eliminate credit card debt, the first step is to determine how much credit card debt you may owe. Once you determine the amount of the debt, specifically state the time frame associated with achieving that particular goal. One credit card might have a balance of $1,800 and it is your goal to completely pay off this debt within 18 months.

When identifying your goals it may be very helpful to set up a grid schedule that will help you organize and manage those goals. Short-term goals represent those that you should plan to accomplish in 1-3 years. Mid-term goals are those that you plan to accomplish within 4-7 years. Long-term goals are those that exceed seven years.

Below is a sample of how this grid should look.

Short-term	Cost	Time	Start Time	Monthly	Action Required
Pay off credit cards	$10,000	24 mo.	Mo. 1	$417	
Savings	$5000	36 mo.	Mo. 6	$125	
Home	$15,000	28 mo.	Mo. 1	$500	
Mid-term					
Colledge	$30,000	72 mo.	Mo. 6	$369	
Business	$5000	48 mo.	Mo. 12	$85	
Buy Land	$15,000	60 mo.	Mo. 15	$204	
Long-term					
Retire	$200,000	180 mo.	Mo. 1	$578	
Travel	$25,000	120 mo.	Mo. 36	$520	
Fund a Trust	$20,000	96 mo.	Mo. 60	$177	

The monthly dollar requirements necessary to meet the established goals should now be incorporated into your monthly budget. By doing this, you can help insure that the proper amounts are set aside to insure that the financial resources will be there to meet the targeted date for achieving the individual goals. As your budget is being developed, you may be required to take certain actions to insure that the monthly requirement can be met. For example, you may need to reduce money spent in certain areas in order to have it available to fund the monthly amounts needed in the aforementioned Grid.

From this grid, you must now write out a detailed plan of action for each goal. When developing this plan, care should be exercised to insure that every specific detail is accounted for. This plan should include the step-by-step process necessary to achieve the goal. For example, if your goal is to start a business, your plan of action should include the following:

- Write a Mission Statement for the business
- List the detailed goals and ojectives for the business
- Prepare a comprehensive business plan with financial projections (engage an expert for this)
- Identify potential funding sources to capitalize the business.
- Name the business.
- Make a decision on the form of entity (Corporation, Partnership, S Corporation, etc.).
- Obtain a tax ID number.
- Open a bank account.
- Do research on the potential market and customer base.
- Determine the need or demand for your product or service.
- Map out how you will deliver your product or service.
- Determine how you will distinguish your business from your competitors.
- Decide on a date to start the business.
- Obtain a location for your business.
- Address personnel needs.

There are many other steps involved in starting a new business. These are just a few of the basics. As with other goals, the process of insuring that each goal is met in a timely fashion requires a carefully mapped out plan. In doing so, you must also determine the resources needed to carry out the plan of action.

Throughout this process it will be helpful to get a partner that will help hold you accountable to your plan of action. This will keep you on task and on course to achieve and exceed your goals.

SETTING PRIORITIES

Since it may be impossible logistically and financially to accomplish all of your goals at the same time, it becomes important to set priorities for which goals are more or less pressing. To help evaluate your priorities, there are several questions you should consider.

List the five uses of your money that have made a positive difference in your life.

1. _____
2. _____
3. _____
4. _____
5. _____

List five uses of your money that have added little quality to your life.

1. _____

2. _____

3. _____

4. _____

5. _____

List five uses of your money that you feel will have a positive affect on your life ten or more years from now.

1. _____

2. _____

3. _____

4. _____

5. _____

List five uses of your money that you feel will have a negative affect on your life ten or more years from now.

1. _____

2. _____

3. _____

4. _____

5. _____

It has been said that if you follow the money (spending habits) you will find where a person's heart lies. As you review your answers to these questions, you will get a clear sense of where you should be directing your resources.

As you chart your course towards achieving your dreams, make sure some basics have been taken care of, or considered.

- Have you developed a good, workable budget that provides for you living on 70% of your net payroll?

- Have you built up an emergency fund of three months net salary?

- Have you addressed those debts with very high interest rates?

- Are your necessities taken of?

- Are there any major life events anticipated over the next three years?

FINAL REMINDERS

Please always consider these final reminders throughout the goal setting process:

- Every financial decision you make can be emotionally driven based on your past. Try to take emotion out of the financial decision and look at the practical aspects of each financial decision.

- Review financial decisions made in the recent pass. Don't dwell on them, but consider what you would have done differently if you had a second opportunity.

- Keep your most important goal in the forefront of your mind. Constantly review your plan of action to accomplish your goal.

- Carry around with you a list of your goals as a reminder that every dollar that is spent on discretionary items directly affects your ability to achieve your dreams in a timely fashion.

- Make sure to separate your short-term goals from your long-term goals. It's difficult to work towards goals that are years into the future. Sometimes you will lose focus and the motivation to achieve your goals.

- Post your goals in different places around the house, like the refrigerator door or a bathroom mirror, where you can be constantly reminded of them.

- Be realistic. Make sure to set goals that can be attained. Your plan of action should show how each goal can be achieved and what resources are needed.

- Update your list of goals often. Changes in your priorities will sometimes have an affect on the order of your goals.

- Make sure you research your goals by discussing them with someone that may have already achieved the same goal. Ask them what it took to achieve their goals.

- Stay focused. Achieving your goal is solely contingent on you carrying out your plan and being consistent.

Chapter 4

PRINCIPLE #3
Live Within Your Means
Develop A Budget

*For which of you, intending to build a tower, does not sit
down first and count the cost, whether he has
enough to finish it...*
Luke 14:28

Budgeting is something we all understand, but few of us actually do. Maybe if we better understood the importance and benefits of budgeting, more of us would do it. An important starting point to developing an effective budget is to determine what your monthly cash flow is. This was discussed in the last chapter. After determining just how you are spending your money, it's time to determine how you should be spending your money. In doing this, consideration must be given to saving and investing to insure that certain future goals are met. In developing a budget, you must identify what the objectives of the budget are. Examples include, making sure you are not living from paycheck to paycheck, making sure your future goals are met and insuring you are spending money for things that build wealth. Also, it is very important to compare your proposed budget with that of a prosperous family.

As mentioned in Chapter I, the rich are getting richer and the poor getting poorer. One reason for this is that the rich are employing sound money management principles. These are the same biblical principles that God intends for us, as Christians, to apply. If sound budgeting is a principle used by the wealthy, then we should be using the same principle. We are wealthy because the Scripture says so. We are the children of a God who created everything and owns everything. We must start acting like the wealthy people we are. We should want God to see us as the "good and faithful" servants He has called us to be. We are stewards of His resources and it is required that we be faithful stewards.

By comparing your budget to that of a guideline budget for a family, certain items might stand out as unusually low or high. Let's take a look at the table below, which reflects the Johnson family's recently unadjusted budget, and compare it to a guideline budget for a family of four with gross income of $40,000 per year. The Johnsons developed this budget after tracking their actual monthly expenditures for an eight month period. The percentages are determined by dividing the average monthly total for each line item by the total expended for the month.

Type of Expense	You	Guideline
Housing	20%	24%
Transportation	10%	8%
Insurance	6%	4%
Food	8%	8%
Entertainment	7%	3%
Church and Charities	4%	10%
Income Taxes	15%	15%
Clothing	7%	3%

Children Related Expense	5%	5%
Debts	10%	3%
Medical	4%	4%
Miscellaneous Expenses	4%	4%
Investments	0%	7%
Emergency Savings	0%	4%

As can be seen from this comparison, it is evident that the Johnson family is not planning for the future since there is no provision for savings or investing. Additionally, too much is being allocated to debts, entertainment, transportation and clothing. These four items exceed the guideline budget by 17 percent. A few percentage points may not seem like a lot. However, when this pattern is repeated for five to ten years, the total effect becomes very substantial. Based on an annual income of $ 40,000, this family is over spending $6,800 in these four areas. Over spending in one area causes neglect in other critical areas, such as tithing, savings, and investing for future goals and dreams.

Nowhere in this budget is it reflected that the Johnson's are paying themselves for the hard work they do throughout the year. We must pay ourselves to keep from becoming frustrated with life. We must be able to show something for our hard work apart from paying everyone else first.

It may seem obvious where the Johnson family is going wrong. However, this type of budget is typical for the majority of Americans. The reason this is the case is that we are so busy trying to keep our heads above water; we can't focus in on the obvious problem. The average family never does this type of analysis. It is probably fair to say that if this analysis had been done and these results were produced, most families would change immediately.

It's not hard to see the impending disaster. If the car needs major repair, the family wants to take a vacation, or one parent is laid off or becomes seriously ill and cannot work, there is no reserve for such emergencies. Money is borrowed or some bills go unpaid and the situation worsens. It becomes a vicious cycle from which it is difficult to escape.

Your first step towards breaking this cycle is to analyze your spending habits and develop a budget that will help move you closer to becoming a prosperous family. Don't try to recover overnight. The change should be gradual, but consistent. Remember, you are breaking old habits. Try to accomplish a budget that reflects the guideline budget within one year (12 months). This analysis should be done monthly until you meet your goal. Thereafter, your budget should be compared to your actual monthly spending to determine if you are adhering to your budget. It will be well worth the effort.

As you can see, budgeting is very important to the process of moving from poverty to prosperity; from getting by to accumulating wealth. The sooner you start to analyze your spending habits, and adjust those habits towards a practical and proven budget formula, the sooner you will be on your way to financial freedom and independence.

In developing an effective budget, you are required to make some very difficult decisions. We often live beyond our resources. In other words, most people are spending too much and saving or investing too little. This type of lifestyle will keep you in financial bondage. It also helps our economy. The United States economy is a capitalist system that is driven by the spending habits of its citizens. The more we spend the healthier the economy becomes.

You will be required to make some drastic adjustments in your spending to create room for savings, investing and dreaming. As a general rule, you should try to live on 70 percent of your net income after taxes. The other 30 percent should be designated for tithes, savings and investing. This will allow you to accumulate an emergency fund, a retirement fund, and a dream fund—all of which will support your goals and dreams.

These decisions may require you to change where you live, temporarily. It may require you to change where you shop and how often you go to the movies or out to dinner. It may require you to start bringing your lunch instead of going out to lunch everyday.

You will be amazed at how much money you spend on things that you really don't need. You have to decide what is actually important to you; what adds value to your life; what's best for your future or your children's future. When these tough decisions are made, you are guaranteed to see positive results.

Some of the adjustments may need to be done step by step. The following worksheet will be helpful to you in this process.

Type of Expense	Budget %	Budget $	Actual $	Diff.
Housing	24%			
Transportation	8%			
Insurance	4%			
Food	8%			
Entertainment	3%			

Church and Charities	10%			
Income Taxes	15%			
Clothing	3%			
Children Related	5%			
Debts	3%			
Medical	4%			
Miscellaneous	4%			
Investments	7%			
Emergency Savings	4%			

Each month this worksheet should be completed until the actual equals the budgeted. Certain rows of expenses in which you are over budget should be targeted for reduction. The newly created savings in those line items will make money become available for other items such as savings, investing, paying down debt, etc. The savings will be the fund that you will use for your primary source to fund your goals.

Remember, money is always working and it will work for you until you spend it. Then, it begins to work for someone else. Always be aware of where you are spending your money. As a rule of thumb, make sure you pay yourself. After all, you are the one earning the wages. Don't work just to pay someone else. By saving and investing your money, you are effectively paying yourself.

Let your goals, dreams and objectives be your motivation to make the tough decisions.

Chapter 5

PRINCIPLE #4
Renew Your Mind About Interest

... so you ought to have deposited my money with the bankers, and at my coming I would have received back my own with interest.
Matthew 25:27

Interest can work for or against you. It can help you achieve financial independence, or drive you to economic and financial ruin. Interest represents the cost for the use of money. If you are using someone else's money (loan), interest is the cost for the use of that money. If someone is using your money (investment), interest is the amount you earn or charge for the use of your money.

INVESTMENTS

Interest can be your friend or foe. When it is working for you, it's safe to say it is your friend. Money is typically working for you through some sort of investment of money. In essence, you are allowing someone else to use your money and you are charging a fee for that privilege. Money is always working, 24 hours a day. It is either working for or against you. The Bible tells us in *Matthew 25:27*, in the parable of the talents, to invest and earn interest on our money. This is a basic principle of money management. The Bible also teaches in Proverbs 22:7 that the lender rules over the borrower.

It becomes increasingly clear that the Lord wants you to be good stewards of His resources that He has entrusted to you, which includes money. Earning interest on money instead of paying interest for money represents good stewardship.

It's never too soon to start thinking about investing. Done wisely, it can help you meet your long term and immediate financial goals: buying a home, paying for a college education, enjoying a comfortable retirement or whatever is important to you.

You don't have to be wealthy to be an investor. Investing even a small amount can produce considerable rewards over the long term if done regularly.

When you invest, you're trying to increase your income and build the value of your assets. Investing means you have to make good, sound decisions about how your money is used. To make wise decisions, you need to clearly understand your options, the risks and the potential rewards.

There are many types of investments. Some of the ones you may have heard of include stocks, bonds, mutual funds, certificates of deposit, and money market funds. Each of these vehicles has its own characteristics, requirements and restrictions. These types of investments will be discussed in greater detail later in this chapter.

MONEY IS ALWAYS WORKING

When investing, it is very important to understand that money is constantly working, 24 hours a day, seven days a week, 365 days a year. The secret is that money only works for the person who owns it. Therefore, it is safe to say that money will work for you as long as you are not spending it for consumable goods and services.

Here are some examples of how money is constantly working.

1. When you deposit money into your checking account it doesn't just sit there until you use it. Your deposits are grouped with monies of other depositors and, in turn, invested by the bank. The bank invests your money by loaning it out to other customers for things like cars and homes. The bank earns profits by charging the borrower interest. If at the end of the day some of the deposits are not invested, the bank will loan money to other banks for their use. This loan, called a reverse repo, is quite common in the banking industry. The bank borrowing the money pays the lending bank a small fee for the use of the money.

2. When you purchase an insurance policy, the premium you pay is grouped with the premiums paid by other insured and invested in various different investment vehicles. It is actually required that excessive cash flow earned by the insurance company be invested and not sit dormant. In order for an insurance company to be in a position to pay claims, it must earn a certain amount of return on its investments.

Not only is it a good business practice to earn a fair return on your investments, but it is also scriptural. In *Matthew 25:27*, Jesus speaks in a parable on steward-ship and specifically makes reference to earning a good interest rate on resources, for which we are stewards.

In the field of finance there is a principal called the **Time Value of Money**. This principal provides that when money is invested consistently (monthly), it grows at a more rapid rate than the same amount invested periodically, withdrawn and re-invested. It's better to invest $100 per month than to invest $200 every other month or $1,200 per year. Since interest is earned daily, any amount invested, including the inter-est that is earned, continues to earn interest. What this means is that not only does the $100 earn interest, but the interest also earns interest. Therefore, the faster you get your money out of your hands and into an invest-ment vehicle the faster it will grow.

The following table shows how money grows with time assuming that you invest $100.00 per month.

Period	8%	12%	15%	18%
5 Yrs.	$ 7,350	$ 8,167	$ 8,857	$ 9,621
10 Yrs.	$ 18,295	$ 23,004	$ 27,522	$ 33,129
15 Yrs.	$ 34,604	$ 49,958	$ 66,851	$ 90,562
20 Yrs.	$ 58,902	$ 98,925	$149,724	$230,885
25 Yrs.	$ 95,103	$187,885	$324,353	$573,725

From this table, you can see that there are two key factors to maximizing your investments: the rate of return and the amount of time.

The Rate of Return earned will have a direct impact on how much you earn and how fast you can grow your investments.

The amount of Time you choose to invest will also have a direct impact on how much you can accumulate in an investment. The longer you consistently invest, the more you can accumulate in your investment vehicle.

Therefore, it is critical to choose the right kind of investment (one that has proven based on past results), to yield the rate of return you desire for your investment. Also, it is key to be consistent with your investing. That means you should try to invest the same amount each and every month. Even if you may experience months that you may not be able to meet the originally committed amount, you should invest something and not lose that months earning potential.

MAKE MONEY WORK FOR YOU

Now that you can see the importance of what you do with your money, it's time to make it work for you. Remember, money is always working—either for you or for someone else. To make money work for you, you must place it where it can earn interest or where you can anticipate a return on your investment. This is known as growth. As can be seen from the above table, the earlier you start money working for you, the more you will accumulate.

The general rule when you are investing is time is your friend. However, when you are only spending and not investing, time can be your enemy. I encourage you to start saving and investing as soon as possible. There is no such thing as starting too soon. Even as a child, it's a great idea to begin investing and doing it consistently. The amount you invest is not as important as the actual act of investing. Changing your behavior about how you handle money is what's important.

Imagine if you started to put $100 a month into a mutual fund for your 5-year-old child and that fund earns 12 percent per year. By the time that child reaches the age of 25, they would have accumulated almost $100,000. During that time you actually would have paid in just $24,000, but because of the theory called the **"Time Value of Money"** or **"Compound Interest"**, your money will grow exponentially. Now, do you think you can find an extra $100 per month?

There is a principle called the **Rule of 72**. It states that if you divide your interest rate earned or rate of return earned into 72, you will get the number of years it will take a one-time investment to double.

For example, if you invested $1,000 into a fund earning 6 percent, it would take 12 years to double your money if you left it there. The table below demonstrates this point.

Interest Rate	Years to Double
3%	24
6%	12
12%	6
18%	4

This table shows just how important the rate of return you receive on your investment is. As the rate of return increases, the number of years it takes for your money to double rapidly shortens. Would you prefer to double your money every 24 years or every 4 years? That is what many would call a no brainer.

Let's look at another example of a one-time

investment of $5,000.00 by a person 29 years old. Take a look at the effect of rate of return on this investment up to retirement age of 65.

Age	6% Return	12% Return	Difference
29	$ 5,000	$ 5,000	0
35		$ 10,000	
41	$ 10,000	$ 20,000	$ 10,000
47		$ 40,000	
53	$ 20,000	$ 80,000	$ 60,000
59		$160,000	
65	$ 40,000	$320,000	$280,000

At age 65, the investment yielding 12 percent grew to $320,000, which is $280,000 more than the investment yielding 6 percent. Even though the rate was double, the actual difference over time is much more than double. Rate of return is the key. You should always strive to maximize your rate of return without exposing your money to a level of uncomfortable risk. Chapter VIII will discuss theory of risk and return. In other words the higher the anticipated return, the higher the potential risk of loss. Each investor must find a level of risk that is acceptable and comfortable.

We all should be motivated to start now. It is never too late or too early. The worst thing you can do is to do nothing. Actually, there is a real cost to waiting.

The following table shows how costly it can be to wait before starting to invest your resources. In this example, one person decides to start investing $100 per month at a rate of return of 10 percent. The others decide to wait until they are 26, 30 and 40 years of age.

Begin Saving At Age	Amount Earned at Age 65	Cost of Waiting
25	$ 637,680	0
26	$ 576,090	$ 61,590
30	$ 382,830	$ 254,850
40	$ 133,790	$ 503,890

As you can see, waiting just one year makes a big difference. Waiting five years could cost you over a quarter of a million dollars. Apply this table to your personal situation and take a look at your investment decisions or lack thereof over the past five to ten years and compute just what has been the cost to you of waiting.

Here's the basic rule of thumb: The sooner you begin saving, the greater the growth potential of your investment. Time, combined with rate of return and consistency, overcomes a million shortcomings. Remember, money is always working. The sooner you invest, the sooner your money will work for your benefit.

Finally, try to contribute or invest as much as you can. Just a little more invested consistently makes a great difference. Let's look at this final table, which demonstrates the difference of investing $20 versus $100 per month at the same rate of return.

Years Invested	Monthly Contribution of $20.00	Monthly Contribution of $100.00	Difference
10	$ 4,130	$ 20,660	$ 16,530
20	$ 15,310	$ 76,570	$ 61,260
30	$ 45,590	$ 227,930	$ 182,340
40	$ 127,540	$ 637,680	$ 510,140

It's hard to imagine that $80 per month could make such a drastic difference. To maximize your return it helps to squeeze out just a little bit more.

There are many types of investments to consider. For many potential investors, the sheer number of choices creates confusion and actually discourages the uninformed investor from entering the market. In Chapter VIII we will discuss the different kinds of investments as well as the pros and cons of each. Because there are so many types of investments and investment strategies, there is certain to be an investment and strategy designed just for you.

Chapter 6

PRINCIPLE #5
Educate Yourself About Debt

The rich rule over the poor,
And the borrower is servant to the lender.
Proverbs 22:7

My people are destroyed for lack of knowledge: because
thou hast rejected knowledge, I will also reject thee,...
Hosea 4:6

Debt is what results when you borrow money from someone, whether an individual or a lending institution. It can take on many forms and is done for many reasons. Listed below is a summary of the various types of debt and the differences between them.

A survey of the average American family indicates that their total average debt, excluding their mortgage, is $16,635. This debt has been the cause of the destruction of many good and loving families, good marriages and businesses with great ideas and products. The payment terms attached to the debt often is not what the borrower thought it was. It normally is much more burdensome on the family's monthly budget than anticipated.

There has been an orchestrated and coordinated plan by banks, finance companies, and insurance companies to get you in this position. Please note that not many banks, insurance companies or credit card companies have gone bankrupt in recent times. The reason why is that their money is made using your money. The more you consume using debt, the more they profit.

The use of credit is a prime driver of the our entire economy, especially in the retail market. The majority of purchases are made using some sort of credit. Imagine what would happen to the retail market if no credit cards were used. The use of these cards is very critical to the survival of many commercial markets. Credit card issuers sometimes add extra privileges to attract customers to their gold or platinum premium cards. The goal is to get you to consume goods and services using either your money or someone else money.

Your buying decision is so important that billions of dollars are spent annually to influence that decision. Think about the number of commercials broadcast on television, radio and the internet. Think about the billboards around the country and the ads in newspapers. Many businesses and industries are dependent on your buying decision. Remember, if your decision to buy was based on the cash you actually have available, your decisions might differ from that of buying with extended credit. In most cases, my rule of thumb is that if you are buying with credit, you are probably buying something you can't afford. That does not matter to the business selling you the products.

Let's walk through a transaction of buying furniture and see who benefits from your buying decision to purchase using credit made available to you.

The Jones family recently moved into their newly purchased home. They have furniture for every room except the dining room. They have $500 saved to purchase furniture for their home. They decided to go to a furniture store to see what they could get for the $500 they have saved. At the store they see the perfect *dining room set, complete with a china cabinet and serving table. Unfortunately, the set cost $2,500. Everyone loved the set, including the salesperson. The furniture store has a special financing arrangement which would allow the Jones to purchase the dining room set with no money down. They would not be required to make a payment until the following year, which is 9 months away. This seems like a great deal, especially since the payments appear to be affordable if they were to adjust their budget just a little. They sign the deal and make the purchase and begin to enjoy their new dining room set.*

The Jones family has just made a financial decision that could negatively impact them for the next five to 10 years. What they did not consider was the terms of the deal they signed. The interest rate was 18.5 percent, and if they are ever late with their payment the rate goes up to 30 percent. In addition, the 9 months that no payments were being made, the obligation was accruing interest at 18.5 percent. As a result, by the time they made their first payment, the Jones actually owed $2,700. If all payments are made on time, the Jones will be paying for that furniture for the next seven years. If there are late payments, that repayment period could be 10 years. Those payments over the entire loan period would exceed $7,000.

Not only has the Jones family spent more than they could afford, they have also paid almost three times the retail price for the furniture. Based on their finances, the Jones actually went shopping for furniture that cost $500, the amount they had saved. The better decision would have been to purchase something for $500 or to continue to save money until they had enough to purchase what they actually wanted. If credit did not exist, they would not have spent $2,500 because they could not afford it. Therefore, their decision to use credit to purchase the furniture caused them to purchase something they could not afford.

Since the Jones did not benefit financially from this decision, lets see who really benefited from the decision.

THE FURNITURE STORE – The owners of the Furniture store purchased the furniture in its showroom at a wholesale price. This price is normally one half the price marked for the consumer (retail price). Therefore when the Jones purchased the furniture, the furniture store made a 100% profit on the sale. Even though the Jones did not pay money directly to the furniture store, by buying on credit they did promise to pay a finance company for the furniture. The finance company actually paid the furniture store on your behalf.

THE SALES PERSON- The sales person that directed you to the dining room set you selected will receive a commission for the sale. That is how they make the majority of their income. The more customers they get to buy furniture, the more commission they make. Also, the more they get each customer to spend the more they make. It does not matter if the customer buys by cash or by credit. The furniture store will pay that commission because they will get their profits from the customer directly (cash *purchase) or indirectly (from the finance company).*

THE FINANCE COMPANY – The finance company benefits from the Jones' purchase because the Jones agreed to pay 18.5% interest to the finance company annually for the money advanced to them to buy the furniture. Over time, the finance company can make almost three times the amount of the loan in interest alone. That is an extremely profitable venture for the finance company.

THE MANUFACTURERS - This is the company that makes the furniture. Typically, if the manufacturer sells the furniture to the store at a wholesale price, then it actually only cost them half that amount to make the furniture. That includes paying for the wood, factory usage, workers to make the furniture and the transportation of the furniture to the furniture store. Also, benefiting from this process are the trucking company, the workers at the plant and the lumberjacks that cut the wood to be used.

Everyone is getting paid, except the Jones. They will be doing the paying over and over again for up to ten years. Know you can see why it is so important that the Jones buy more than they can afford. There are so many direct and indirect beneficiaries from their purchase. Imagine this multiplied by millions. That is the reality of this scenario because there are millions of other consumers just like the Jones. Don't be like the Jones.

As a general rule and a biblical based stewardship principle, you should owe man nothing but love. The bible also teaches us that the borrower is a servant to the lender. Therefore do your best to not incur any unnecessary debt without carefully considering the cost associated with that debt. Make sure there is good reason for incurring the debt and that you are not just buying something you cannot afford.

There may be times when you need money for something that requires an immediate cash outlay, such as to buy a car, pay college tuition, make repairs to or renovate your home. You are now faced with the decision of how much to borrow, what type of loan to take and what should be the terms of the loan. If you know how different types of loans work and the particular features they offer, you will be in a better position to look for the one that will be best suited for you. With this knowledge, you can avoid the debt trap that so many Americans find themselves in.

LOANS

There are many types of loans that charge interest to the borrower. They include credit cards, installment loans, charge cards, mortgage loans, business loans, investment loans, lines of credit, revolving loans, fixed rate loans, and adjustable rate loans. Along with interest, there are other related charges that are charged to the borrower. Individuals borrow money in the form of loans to enable them to purchase certain goods that they either cannot or choose not to pay for at the time of receiving the goods. Too often, we borrow money to purchase goods we can't afford to pay for at the time. From a consumers' perspective, using credit means buying now and paying later. Credit is typically used to purchase the following items:

- Cars
- Homes
- Home Improvements
- Vacations
- Furniture
- Clothes
- Appliances
- Entertainment
- Starting a Business
- Consolidation of Loans
- Other Goods and Services

There are various types of companies that lend money and there are advantages and limitations for each type of company. These companies include commercial banks, savings and loans, credit unions, finance companies, insurance companies, credit card companies, and brokerage firms. The table below summarizes the advantages and limitations for each type of company.

Lenders	Types	Advantages	Limitations
Banks	Home improvement, education, personal, auto, mobile home	• Widely available locations and funds • Preferred rates for bank customers • Loans often cost less than at commercial banks	• Require good credit rating • Higher rates than some other sources • Exist in only some states
Credit Unions	Home improvement, personal loans, auto	• Can be easy to arrange for members in good standing • Lowest rates	Membership required in organization or group
Financing Company	Auto, appliance (major), boat, mobile home	Can be easy to arrange good terms during special promotions	• High rates • Since loans are secured, defaulting can mean loss of the item and the payments already made
Small Loan Company	Auto, personal	• Can be easy to arrange • Good credit rating not required	• High rates • Cosigner often required
Insurance Company	General purpose	May be able to borrow up to 95% of policy's surrender value	• Outstanding loan plus interest reduce payment to survivors • Policy ownership is required
Brokers	Margin account, general purpose loans, using investments as security	• Can be easy to arrange (with little delay in getting money) • Low rates (but subject to change) • Flexible repayment	• Changing value of investments may require payment of additional security • Margin requirements may change

Or course, in some ways all loans are alike. The money you borrow is called the **principal**, and you agree to pay it back over a specific term, or length of time, with **interest**. The conditions and terms of the loan, some of which are listed below, will affect how much you can borrow and how much the loan will cost you.

SELECTED TERMS AND CONDITIONS

Below we will explore the definitions and explanations of key terms and conditions such as:

- Whether you pay in installments or return the lump sum

- Whether the interest is fixed or adjustable
- Whether the loan is secured or unsecured

INSTALLMENT LOANS

When you take an installment loan, you borrow the money all at once and repay it in set amounts, or installments, on a regular schedule, usually once a month. Installment loans are also called closed-end loans because you must pay them off by a specific date.

For example, if you take a five-year $20,000 loan at 10% interest:

Monthly payments for 5 years	$424.96
Total payment	$25,497.60
Total interest paid	$5,497.60

SECURED LOANS

Your loan is secured when you put up security or collateral to guarantee it. The lender can sell the collateral if you fail to repay the loan in accordance with the terms and conditions of the loan. Automobile loans and home equity loans are the most common types of secured loans.

UNSECURED LOANS

An unsecured loan is made solely on your promise to repay. If the lender thinks you are a good credit risk, nothing but your signature is required. However, the lender may require a cosigner, who promises to repay the loan if you don't. Since unsecured loans pose a bigger risk for lenders, they may have higher interest rates and stricter conditions.

In 1856, Isaac Singer introduced the concept of buying on time or paying for something while you're using it as a way to sell his sewing machines. At $5 down and $5 a month, the average family could afford a $125 machine otherwise impossible on a typical $500 annual income.

ADJUSTABLE INTEREST RATE

An adjustable-rate loan has a variable interest rate. When the rate changes, usually every six months or once a year, the monthly payment also changes.

Advantages:
- Initial rate lower than fixed rate
- Lower overall costs if rates drop
- Annual increases usually controlled

Disadvantages:
- Vulnerable to rate hikes
- Hard to budget increases
- Not always available

FIXED INTEREST RATE

Many installment loans have a fixed rate. The interest rate and the monthly payments stay the same for the entire term or length of the loan.

Advantages:

- Installments stay the same

- Easy to budget payments

- The cost of the loan does not increase

- No surprises

Disadvantages:

- Interest remains the same, even if market rates decrease

- Initially higher interest rates than an adjustable rate loan

LINE OF CREDIT

A personal line of credit is a type of **revolving credit.** This type of credit allows you to write special checks for the amount you want to borrow, up to a limit set by the lender. The credit doesn't cost you anything until you write a check. Then you begin to pay interest on the amount you borrowed. You must repay at least a minimum amount each month plus interest, but you can repay more, or even the whole loan amount, whenever you want. The amount you repay becomes available for you to borrow again.

Banks and credit issuers sometimes offer lines of credit automatically to people they consider good customers. But that doesn't mean you have to use them if you prefer not to.

For example, if you have a $10,000 line of credit, you have access to that money over and over, as long as you repay what you use:

$10,000	Line of credit
- $ 6,000	You borrow
= $4,000	Available credit
+ $1,000	You repay
= $5,000	Available credit

Advantages:

- Only one application

- Instant access to credit

Disadvantages:

- Potentially high interest rates

- Easy to over-borrow

THE COST OF A LOAN

The three things that will determine what borrowing will cost you are the finance charge, lender fees and the length of the loan.

The cheapest loan is not the one with the lowest payments, or the lowest interest rate. Instead, you have to look at the total cost of borrowing, which depends on the interest rate plus fees, and the term, or length of time it takes you to repay. While you probably can't influence the rate and fees, you may be able to arrange for a shorter term or repayment period.

SELECTED FEES FOR LOANS

Application fees cover processing expenses.

Attorney fees pay the lender's attorney. Your attorney fees are extra.

Credit search fees cover researching your credit history.

Origination fees cover administrative costs and appraisal fees.

THE COST OF TAKING LONGER TO REPAY

The term of your loan is crucial when determining total cost of the loan. Shorter terms mean squeezing larger amounts into fewer payments. But it also means you'll pay interest for fewer years, which saves you a lot of money.

Consider for example, the interest for three different terms on a $13,500 car loan at 12.5 percent.

	3 Years	4 Years	5 Years
Payments	36	48	60
Payment Amount	$451.62	$358.82	$303.72
Total Repaid	$16,258.32	$17,223.36	$18,223.20
Total Interest Paid	$2,758.32	$3,723.36	$4,723.20

LOAN REPAYMENT

The borrower will write a check for the same amount each time and the payment will always cover a different proportion of principal and interest.

From the first check written to repay a loan, a certain amount goes to pay the interest, and the rest goes to repay the money borrowed or the principal.

The chart below shows how a $100,000 mortgage loan is amortized, or paid off, over the life of a 30-year repayment period with a 7 percent interest rate. Notice how the borrower gradually shifts from paying mostly interest in the early years to paying mostly principal in the later years. That's because lenders **front-load** their interest charges to guarantee their profit. In other words, instead of spreading the interest evenly over the life of the loan, they collect most of the interest first. While most other installment loans have much shorter terms than that of a mortgage, the repayment process is similar.

Term (Months)	Dates	Loan Balance	Principal	Interest	Total Monthly Payment
	Jan. 2000	$100,000	N/A	N/A	N/A
	Apr. 2000	$99,669	$83.10	$581.89	$665.33
60	Jan. 2005	$95,362	$115.52	$549.78	$665.33
120	Jan. 2010	$85,813	$163.77	$501.53	$665.33
180	Jan. 2015	$75,311	$232.16	$433.14	$665.33
240	Jan. 2020	$60,803	$329.12	$336.18	$665.33
300	Jan. 2025	$38,565	$466.57	$198.73	$665.33
360	Jan. 2030	$0	$661.42	$3.88	$665.33

CREDIT CARDS

Credit Cards are used to make the majority of purchases for consumer goods and services. Credit cards give you revolving access to a fixed sum of money. This means that as soon as you've repaid the amount you have used, you can use it again. Creditors are willing and often eager to advance you the principal, or the amount you use, because they collect a fee called a finance charge as you repay.

When used properly, credit cards can provide a tremendous benefit, such as convenience. When used for business purposes such as travel and entertainment, credit cards are a very practical and convenient way of paying for goods and services. Typically, since credit cards used for business purposes are used for convenience, the amount charged is paid off monthly. Therefore, no finance charges are incurred or such finance charges are kept to a minimum.

Credit cards are also very convenient for personal use in certain circumstances. For example, when traveling it is practical to pay for hotel rooms and other related expenses with a credit card. The amount expended should be limited to a budgeted amount that will be repaid within one month. Therefore, the credit card is used instead of cash. This would keep you from the risk of carrying large sums of cash around.

BEFORE CREDIT CARDS

Layaway plans, which were once common, would allow you to pay a small amount each week against the purchase price of items such as clothing or furniture, which the merchant would hold until you paid the entire cost. But if winter came before you finished paying for your coat, you'd still be cold.

Department stores provide **charge cards** that let you make purchases within that particular store and make monthly payments to the store. In the past, you generally had to pay in full or you could no longer use the card. Today, however, most charge cards work like credit cards, though they're still limited to a single retailer or affiliation of stores.

Many retailers in the United States and around the world accept both credit cards and travel and entertainment cards, while some accept only one or the other. In fact, most of the major cards are so widely accepted that they have reduced your need for separate cards for different retailers and the hassle of multiple bills.

ARTHUR MORRIS originated the installment loan. His Morris Plan, the first to make credit available to the average citizen, began in 1916 despite common wisdom that lending money to working people was doomed to failure. Today, it's hard to imagine how the American economy could function without credit.

CREDIT ASSOCIATIONS

Visa and MasterCard are not-for-profit associations that were created to handle the mechanics of credit card transactions. They are owned by member banks that actually issue the cards and make money on the fees generated when you use them to make purchases. Some banks offer both cards, and some offer one or the other. The average American typically carries from one to three credit cards, and owes about $2,000. Combined, Americans owe about $600 billion in outstanding credit card balances.

Creditors are willing, and often eager, to advance you the money for your use because they collect a fee, called a finance charge, every month the loan remains unpaid. Creditors figure the finance charge by adding a percentage of the principal to the amount you owe. The percentage, called the interest rate, varies depending on the type of credit you're using and the amount of competition the creditor has in attracting your business. It's often linked to the interest rates that are current in the economy at large, particularly the prime rate, which lenders use as a benchmark rate. In general, finance charges on credit cards are figured at a higher, sometimes much higher, rate than those on most loans.

Other factors involved in computing your finance charges include your credit reputation and other assumptions a potential creditor makes about you. If a creditor believes there's a risk that you may default, or fail to repay the loan in a timely fashion, the rate you'll have to pay for credit may be higher than someone who seems to pose less risk.

COMPUTING FINANCE CHARGES

The interest you owe depends on the method used to calculate your finance charge. The three primary methods to compute finance charges are the adjusted, average daily, and previous balance methods. For example, suppose you pay an 18 percent annual finance charge (1.5 percent per month) on amounts you owe. Your previous balance is $2,000, and you pay $1,000 on the 15th day of a 30-day period:

Method	Description	Interest
Adjusted Balance	The company subtracts the amount of your payment from the beginning balance and charges you interest on the remainder. This method cost you the least.	$15.00
Average Daily Balance	The company charges you interest on the average of the amount you owe each day during the period. So the larger the payment you make, the lower the interest you pay.	$22.50

Previous Balance	The company does not subtract any payments you make from your previous balance. You pay interest on the total amount you owe at the beginning of the period. This method costs you the most.	$30.00

Three things affect your card-based credit costs: annual fees, finance charges, and grace periods. You can control your card-based credit costs even if you use credit all the time by choosing a card that's suited to your usage and payment habits. However, if you always have a big outstanding balance and pay only the minimum charges each month, you'll be saddled with huge costs no matter which card you use.

THE COSTS TO CONSIDER

In shopping for a credit card, you'll want to consider the following three costs. They may not control your decision about which card to use, but they can help save you money.

Annual fees are yearly charges for using a particular card. You can often avoid these charges entirely by choosing a card that guarantees that there will be no annual fee for as long as you use it.

Finance charges are the costs of using credit. Many issuers still charge 18 percent or more a year (1.5 percent a month) on the outstanding balances and cash advances, though the justification for those rates come from a period of high inflation in the early 1980s. However, some banks charge less, sometimes significantly less, during an introductory period. If you regularly have an outstanding balance it can be wise to shop for the lowest rate.

Grace period, sometimes called grace days, is the time between the billing date and the required payment date. However, some cards with low interest rates began to charge interest on all purchases from the day they're made, even if you paid your last balance in full. If you always pay on time, you'll probably agree that avoiding interest charges altogether outweighs finding the lowest rate, so be sure to read the small print.

EXTRA COSTS

In addition to an annual fee, card issuers may charge extra fees for specific situations. For example, if you exceed your credit line, you may have to pay an **over limit fee** (usually about $25), even if your charge has been approved. Also, if your minimum payment is overdue there's often a **late payment fee** of about $25. You will probably have to pay a **cash advance fee** for withdrawing money from an automated teller machine (ATM) with your credit card, plus interest for the time between the advance and when you pay it off. Or, you can debit or take money directly out of your checking account with an American Express card for an access fee of 3 percent of the withdrawal ($3 minimum) if you're enrolled in their Express Cash program.

SECURED CREDIT CARDS

If you have trouble getting a credit card, as you might if you have no credit history, no regular job, or you've had financial problems in the past, you may be able to arrange for a **secured card** by opening a savings account and keeping a balance equal to your credit line. If you don't keep up your payments, the bank can take what you owe from the savings account. However, if you use the card regularly–and repay what you owe–you may qualify for a regular card and a higher line of credit.

The use of credit cards becomes damaging when they are abused. This happens when credit cards are used to purchase goods and services that you are unable to afford at the time of purchasing the goods and services. A good test to determine if you can afford the purchase is as follows:

1. You should be able to purchase the items for cash and such purchases must be within your budget.

2. The use of the credit card is only for convenience.

3. The amount paid can be immediately repaid when the credit card bill arrives.

Unfortunately, many people have a tendency to abuse the use of credit cards. All credit cards come with a dollar limit of how much can be purchased with the cards. Most consumers expend up to the maximum dollar limit. Instead of paying down the outstanding balance, they apply for and receive a new credit card and begin to use and abuse it also. This happens again and again until the use of credit cards become a normal way of life. Instead of using credit as a means of convenience, they become dependent on them to maintain their current standard of living and to pay for their normal day-to-day living expenses.

This will always result in financial ruin. It is not

until things have gotten out of control that most people recognize the dire financial position they are in. They then wonder how they got to where they are and more importantly how can they get out of it. If that is you, then you're not alone. The majority of Americans are in similar circumstances.

It has been demonstrated in many case studies that debt is seldom handled properly. Most people who get into debt find their selves over extended. They have incurred more debt than they have the ability to manage. Their monthly payments only cover the interest on the debt. It seldom reduces the principle.

Debt is the primary cause of most Americans financial struggles. This hunger for debt is fed by an unlimited desire to consume. If you want to obtain financial success and financial independence, you must start by eliminating debt from your lives. When you are paying from 8 percent to 18 percent interest to a creditor, it doesn't matter that your investments are earning 10 percent to 12 percent. All the growth in your investments and savings are being eaten up by the interest on your debt.

Strive to minimize and ultimately eliminate all debt from your life. If you have debt outstanding, make sure it is used to purchase something that grows or appreciates at a rate higher than the interest rate you are paying for the debt. Eliminating debt is a clear indication and a sure sign of good stewardship as required in the word of God.

PRINCIPLE #6
Eliminate Debt Out Of Your Life

*Owe no man any thing, but to love one another:
for he that loveth another hath fulfilled the law.*
Romans 13:8

Getting out of debt seems to be the common objective for everyone seeking to gain financial independence. Uncontrollable debt is one of the primary financial problems that causes most people to remain in poverty.

There are 10 basic steps to eliminating debt from your life forever.

1. Resolve to spend less than you make (no more than 70 percent of your net after tax income).

2. Change your spending habits to insure that you will incur no more debt.

3. Realize how much debt you have and what it is costing you to maintain.

4. Adjust your monthly budget to create a cash surplus to be used to accelerate payment of outstanding debt.

5. Target the debt that costs the most in terms of interest rate being paid.

6. Start paying as much as possible towards the principle on your largest debts.

7. Continue making at least the minimum payments on all other debts, paying more whenever possible.

8. Contact creditors to see if interest rates associated with each debt can be reduced.

9. Once one bill is paid in full, apply the money that went towards that bill to the monthly payment your are making on another bill.

10. Consolidate debt wherever possible.

Type of Loan	Amount Owed	Interest Rate	Minimum Mo. Payment	Adjusted Months to Payoff	Required Payment
VISA	5,000	18 %	85.00	18	
Sears	3,500	21%	55.00	12	
Student Loan	8,500	5%	125.00	24	
Car Loan	23,000	14%	525.00	36	
Macys	7,200	17.5%	105.00	12	

For many families, their first attempt at eliminating debt is a mortgage consolidation loan. In this case the family will either refinance the mortgage on their home or take out a second mortgage. Usually, this is not a bad approach. However, when making such a decision it is important to consider all the relative cost.

Usually, there will be closing costs associated with any loan. Additionally, consideration should be given to the term of the loan and the interest rate. Consideration should also be given to making the new loan a 15-year loan instead of the traditional 30-year mortgage.

It may not be wise to take out a loan for the maximum amount. With the real estate market experiencing such a boom, the market value of many homes are soaring. This allows the mortgage company to write large mortgages.

For example, a family has a home that cost $150,000 10 years ago. They now owe $120,000 on the mortgage with an interest rate of 8 percent. The current value of the home is $325,000. Many mortgage companies will loan 90 percent of the value of the home, or $292,500. This would allow the family to pay off the existing mortgage of $120,000 and still have $172,500 before closing cost. This mortgage may be very affordable, considering today's interest rates of 4 to 5 percent. However, if the family only has existing credit card and other debt of $25,000, they will end up with a considerable amount of extra money, which could result in problems for the family. If the family does not exercise good fiscal management, the excess funds will be quickly spent without creating anything of value.

Always have a plan of action for the proceeds from the new mortgage before you acquiring the mortgage. Consideration could be given to investing into a fund that will provide a return greater than the interest rate being paid on the mortgage. If you do not have a well thought out plan, then consider taking out the mortgage only for the amount needed to consolidate your debts. The extra cash can give you a false sense of security and cause you not to adjust your spending habits or make the decisions necessary to become a better steward.

The success of our nations' economy relies heavily on our being active consumers. Many industries are kept viable as a result of our buying habits. As a matter of fact, it is actually important that we incur debt when we buy certain products. As mentioned earlier, we buy goods and services on credit primarily because we cannot afford to pay cash for them. We will try to convince ourselves that we are simply using our credit cards for convenience. In truth, if we were making our buying decisions based solely on the actual cash we have to spend our decisions would change dramatically.

That is why there are so many advertisements enticing consumers to buy now and pay later. Sometimes the ads promise that no payments are required for more than a year. The intent is to encourage you to buy something now that you can't afford so that the profits made from the manufacturing to the retail selling of that product can be realized.

This can be demonstrated by looking at the process of selling a car. Dealers advertise vehicles for no money down, or 1 percent interest. These ads are designed to attract consumers to the show room. Expert car salesman are there waiting to convince you that you need a car and that you can afford the car that you really did not intend to buy.

We must understand who it is that really benefits when a car is sold. Below is listed those who will actually benefit from a car being sold:

- The car dealer will profit from selling the car.

- The manufacturer will profit from selling the car to the dealer.

- The rubber industry benefits from the tires on the car that was sold.

- The steel industry benefits from the steel used to make the car that was sold.

- The plastic industry benefits.

- The newspaper benefits from the ad placed and the new ads to be placed because they work.

- The insurance industry benefits from the new insurance placed on the car.

- The oil and gas industry will benefit from a new car now on the road with a life of at least 5 years (finance period).

- The bank or finance company will benefit from the interest to be earned on the new loan used to finance the car.

- The repair shops benefit from the maintenance required to keep a car running.

There are many other industries that go into the making and selling of a car. None of these industries or their employees would have benefited if you did not buy that car.

Because this one transaction has such a far-reaching effect, great effort and resources are spent to insure that you will be an active consumer. The entire economy depends on that. For this to work, you must buy what you can't afford and it must appear to be painless and normal. Approximately 90 percent of all advertisements are designed to entice you to buy some good or service. Billions of dollars are spent to insure that you actively consume and that you incur debt in doing so.

You must be aware of this and better understand the nature and intent of advertising. Our decisions to consume must be practical and based on an actual need. Your buying decision must make financial sense. Emotion should never be part of the equation. Always make financial decisions based on your budget and your available expendable cash.

Chapter 8

PRINCIPLE #7
Build Wealth With Every Decision

*Beloved, I wish above all things that thou mayest prosper
and be in good health, even as thy soul prospereth.*
3 John 1:2

*But thou shalt remember the Lord thy God: for it is he that giveth
thee power to get wealth, that he may establish his covenant...*
Deuteronomy 8:18

Wealth is a term that has many different meanings. Many define wealth as being a millionaire. Some define it as having more than enough. Some consider it as being financially secure or independent. Wealth cannot be defined with a number because it means different things to different people.

Wealth is a measure of value or worth. When trying to determine your current state of financial affairs, it is very important to measure your net worth. Since it actually represents value, net worth is key.

Earning a million dollars does not make one a millionaire, nor does it dictate wealth. If a person earns $100,000 and spends $40,000, they actually have net cash of $60,000. However, if a person earns $1 million, but spends $1,050,000, they have generated a loss. It is how you manage your resources that will create lasting value.

Net worth is measured by having more assets (things) than liabilities (debts). If you have more assets than liabilities, then you have created net worth or value. Now, as financial decisions are made to buy certain items, the question must be asked, "Have I created anything of value, or have I increased my net worth?"

The three ways to increase net worth are to increase assets, reduce liabilities, and/or a combination of both. If money is spent on entertainment as opposed to investing in a mutual fund, an opportunity to increase net worth would have been missed and wasted.

Emphasis must also be placed on the type of assets being purchased. Some assets grow or increase in value over time. That is why it is vitally important that you understand investing and that you practice controlled and educated investing. Though there are many types of investments with varying levels of risk and return, we will focus on some of the basic types.

STOCKS

By investing in stocks, you are effectively investing in the company that is selling the stock. Companies sell or issue stock to raise money for such things as expansion, debt reduction, research, operations, etc. Stocks of most midsize and large companies are sold (traded) on one of the nation's stock exchanges: the New York Stock Exchange, American Stock Exchange, NASDAQ Stock Market and NASDAQ Small-Cap Market. Once the stock is originally sold, it can be resold to anyone through one of the stock exchanges. The size of the company, and the number of shares issued, determines which exchange the security is traded on.

The price of the stock may change from time to time based on a number of factors such as the economy, the management of the company, developments in the industry, the success of the company, demand for the stock, among other market factors.

When you're choosing stocks from among the thousands that are available in the U.S. and around the world, you can narrow your choices in many ways. Some people buy shares in the company they work for. Other investors concentrate on companies they know, either because they're local firms or because they provide products and service the investor use. Still others make investments in large well known companies and others in companies that are just emerging as leaders in a new field.

Another choice you will need to make when investing in stocks is whether you're seeking income or growth and whether you prefer aggressive or conservative investments. Income stocks are those companies that focus on paying a portion of their earnings back to the investors (shareholders) in the form of a dividend periodically throughout the year. Growth oriented companies focus on reinvesting their earnings back into the company and thereby creating additional value to the stock being held by the shareholders. Younger investors desiring to capitalize of the time value of money should invest in **growth oriented stocks**. Other investors such as retired individuals needing to supplement their income should invest in **income-oriented stocks**.

Aggressive stocks are those that generally seek to generate a higher than normal rate of return. Along with this higher desired return comes a higher than normal level of risk for loss. It is important to note that there is no guarantee that a stock's value will increase. It may decrease and when it does, you lose money. I will speak more about risk and reward later in this chapter.

BONDS

Bonds are another type of investment that allows investors to earn a return on their investments. Bonds are also issued to allow companies to raise capital for various reasons. They are also used by Cities, States and Municipalities to raise money for various reasons (road building, infrastructure, etc.). By investing in these securities, the investor is loaning the company or government money. The Company or Government guarantees the investor that at the end of a particular period they will repay the investor the amount invested along with a fee for using the money. This fee is the investor's return on the investment.

REAL ESTATE

Investing in real estate can range from owning your home to being a partner in a major construction project, from the purchase of an empty wooded lot to owning a castle in France. If you leverage or borrow money to pay for your investment, selling at a profit can mean a healthy return. But leveraging can also magnify your losses should your prices go down. A primary appeal to real estate investing is that over time, prices often dramatically increase, even though at times it can be hard to sell, especially at the price you want.

Positives To Real Estate Investing:
- Provides a hedge against inflation.
- Permits tax deductions in some cases
- Produce big profits in some markets

Negatives To Real Estate Investing:

- Can be difficult to get investment back

- May be overpriced in some markets and undervalued in others

- Subject to zoning laws and environmental issues

CERTIFICATE OF DEPOSITS

A certificate of deposit (or a CD), is an investment issued by banks that allows you to put money into a bank for a specific time and after that time has passed to get the money back plus interest. One of the first things you look for in a CD is the interest rate. This will determine how much you will earn on your money. This type of investment is considered to be one of the safest. For that reason, the rate of return (interest rate) is normally very low as compared to other investments like stocks and bonds. CDs are normally purchased in increments of $500.00. There normally is no ceiling. The specific time period for the CD to mature ranges from 6 months to five years.

At maturity, you must tell the bank in writing what you want them to do with your investment. You can receive the cash, roll it over into the same type of CD or invest in a new CD with a different term and rate.

Rewards of CDs:

- The yield is higher than savings accounts

- Allows you to plan for the future

- There are no charges to you for a CD

- Your bank investment is insured up to $100,000

Risk of CDs:

- Your money is locked at a specific rate, even if rates increase

- You must pay a penalty if you take your money out early

- You can earn more with non-bank investments

- The interest rate may decrease when you roll it over

MUTUAL FUNDS

When you put your money into a mutual fund, it is pooled with other investors' money and used to make investments selected by a fund manager. A good fund manager will seek to earn good returns consistently. To do this, they invest your money in many types of investments. This is called diversification. This means that even if some of the investments are performing worst than expected, others are apt to perform better than expected. A typical mutual fund might own stock in 100 different companies in varying industries.

It is important when buying a mutual fund to determine the track record of the fund and the fund manager over at least a five-year period. When analyzing a mutual fund, you should look for the following:

Performance—How much the fund returns,

whether the returns are consistent and how they compare to other funds.

Risk—How likely you are to earn or lose money. Risk is not always bad, if you are investing for the long-term.

Cost—If you are charged a high commission by your broker, that means less money goes toward your investment.

There are many types of funds for investment. It is important that you have a good working understanding of what these funds are and what the objective and risk of each type of fund is. Below is a chart on types of funds along with fund objective and related risk.

Type Of Fund	Objective	Risk
Aggressive-growth funds invest in new companies and industries and those that are in financial trouble.	Above-average price increase	Volatile and speculative
Growth funds invest in well-established companies whose earnings are expected to increase.	Strong price increases	Can be volatile
Equity funds invest in companies that consistently pay good dividends and also have strong growth potential.	Current income and long-term price increases	Less volatile
Income funds invest in income-producing securities such as dividend-paying stocks, bonds or a combination.	Current income	Less volatile
Balanced funds invest in a mix of bonds, preferred stock and common stock.	Current income and some growth	Less volatile
International funds invest in overseas markets. Global funds invest both in international and U.S. markets.	Profit from strong markets aboard.	Risk of currency fluctuations
Bond funds invest in government, corporate or tax exempt bonds with different maturities.	Current income	Moderate risk
High-yield funds invest in low rated corporate bonds. Tax-free high yield funds invest in lower-rated municipal bonds.	Very high current income	High risk
Money market funds buy short-term government and corporate debt. Many offer check writing privileges.	Income based on current interest rates	Nearly total safety

Of course investing isn't for everyone. But you must understand that if your money isn't working for you it is working for someone else. Remember, increasing assets and/or decreasing liabilities create wealth.

Therefore, if building wealth is a primary goal of yours, which it should be, then every financial decision you make (especially outside of your established monthly operating budget), should contribute toward building wealth. If not you must justify why that decision doesn't contribute towards building wealth. This process will cause you to make much wiser decisions with your money. It gives your spending a real purpose.

Chapter 9

Help Break The Generational Curse

*Train up a child in the way he should go:
and when he is old he will not depart from it.*
Proverbs 22:6

As stewards, we are commanded to be faithful. Consistently applying the principles in this book will help you become a faithful steward so that you experience financial success. But, it doesn't stop there.

We must pass this knowledge on to our children. God has entrusted the training of these precious ones to us, and we must be faithful to this mandate. We must insure that our children understand these biblical principles and begin to apply them to their lives at an early age.

This book demonstrates the benefit of building wealth and the ease in which it can be accomplished if good decisions are made and certain processes applied on a consistent basis. Investing a little over a long period of time will bring great rewards. Remember, the earlier you start investing and saving with your children, the better off they will be when they begin their lives as adults.

Imagine if when you graduated from college and started to work you had a trust fund of $300,000. Do you think that might have made life a little better or enabled you to bless someone else? Money is not the key to happiness, but in this day and age and in our society it is absolutely necessary. Having sufficient resources (like money), can make life and overcoming some of its challenges much easier.

One area to focus on when teaching your children about finances and prosperity is the renewing of the mind. We must change our thinking to incorporate the following mandates:

- Plan to prosper because God wants us to prosper.

- Understand that you have a great amount of control over your financial destiny.

- Know your adversary and his plan to keep you in poverty so that you can't be effective for the Kingdom of God.

- Understand the spiritual implications involved.

- Educate yourself so that you can make informed decisions.

- Remember that cash is king. Strive to generate net positive cash flow to allow your choices to plan your prosperity.

- Define wealth to be net worth and strive to always increase your net worth.

- Be goal driven so that you will always have the motivation to stay focus.

Finally, memorize, understand and apply the

following financial and biblical principles to your life:

- Everything belongs to God.
- God expects us to be good and faithful stewards.
- Create wealth in your life to benefit the Kingdom of God.
- Develop the right attitude about money.
- Be faithful with what you have, no matter how small.
- Get your priorities in proper order.
- Learn how to manage the other 90% (10% belong to God).
- Learn to live on 70% of your income.
- Avoid surety. Don't co-sign for someone else's debt.
- Get out of debt as soon as possible.
- Diversify your assets to lessen the risk.
- Create a cash surplus in your monthly budget.
- Create a short-term and long-term plan and follow it.
- Be honest and operate with integrity.
- Eliminate wasteful spending.
- Train your children on financial matters.
- Help others out of financial bondage.

Let us all strive to teach our children these valuable biblical principles for financial success, how to apply them to their lives and how to continue to pass on this knowledge to many generations to come. God will be glorified.

Appendix I

Deuteronomy 8:18
But thou shalt remember the Lord thy God for it is he that giveth thee Power to get wealth that he may establish his covenant which he sware unto thy fathers as it is this day

Psalm 37:25
I have been young and now I am old, yet I have not seen the righteous abandoned or his children begging bread.

Proverbs 13:22
A good man leaveth an inheritance to his children's children: and the wealth of the sinner is laid up for the just.

Hosea 4:6
My people are destroyed for lack of knowledge: because thou hast rejected knowledge, I will also reject thee, that thou shalt be no priest to me: seeing thou hast forgotten the law of thy God, I will also forget thy children.

Matthew 25:20-21
And so he that had received five talents came and brought other five talents, saying, Lord, thou deliveredst unto me five talents: behold, I have gained beside them five talents more. His lord said unto him, Well done, thou good and faithful servant: thou hast been faithful over a few things, I will make thee ruler over many things: enter thou into the joy of thy lord.

Luke 16:10
He that is faithful in that which is least is faithful also in much: and he that is unjust in the least is unjust also in

much. If therefore ye have not been faithful in the unrighteous mammon, who will commit to your trust the true riches? And if ye have not been faithful in that which is another man's, who shall give you that which is your own?

I Chronicles 29:11-12
Thine, O LORD, is the greatness, and the power, and the glory, and the victory, and the majesty: for all that is in the heaven and in the earth is thine; thine is the kingdom, O LORD, and thou art exalted as head above all. Both riches and honour come of thee, and thou reignest over all; and in thine hand is power and might; and in thine hand it is to make great, and to give strength unto all.

I Corinthian 4:2
Moreover it is required in stewards, that a man be found faithful.

Psalms 50:10-12
For every beast of the forest is mine, and the cattle upon a thousand hills. I know all the fowls of the mountains: and the wild beasts of the field are mine.

Matthew 6:33
But seek ye first the kingdom of God, and his righteousness; and all these things shall be added unto you.

Proverbs 22:6
Train up a child in the way he should go: and when he is old, he will not depart from it. The rich ruleth over the poor, and the borrower is servant to the lender.

Proverbs 24:3-4
A house is built by wisdom and becomes strong through good

sense. Through knowledge its rooms are filled with all sorts
of precious riches and valuables.

II Kings 20:1
In those days was Hezekiah sick unto death. And the prophet
Isaiah the son of Amoz came to him, and said unto him, Thus
saith the LORD, Set thine house in order; for thou shalt die,
and not live.

Genesis 41:34-36
Let Pharaoh appoint officials over the land, and let them
collect one-fifth of all the crops during the seven good years.
Have them gather all the food and grain of these good years
into the royal storehouses, and store it away so there will
be food in the cities. That way there will be enough to eat
when the seven years of famine come. Otherwise disaster
will surely strike the land, and all the people will die."

III John 1:2
Beloved, I wish above all things that thou mayest prosper
and be in good health, even as thy soul prospereth.

Proverbs 22:7
The rich ruleth over the poor, and the borrower is servant to
the lender.

Deuteronomy 28:1-2
And it shall come to pass, if thou shalt hearken diligently unto
the voice of the LORD thy God, to observe and to do all his
commandments which I command thee this day, that the LORD
thy God will set thee on high above all nations of the earth: And
all these blessings shall come on thee, and overtake thee, if thou
shalt hearken unto the voice of the LORD thy God.

Deuteronomy 28:12

The LORD shall open unto thee his good treasure, the heaven to give the rain unto thy land in his season, and to bless all the work of thine hand: and thou shalt lend unto many nations, and thou shalt not borrow.

Exodus 22:25

If thou lend money to any of my people that is poor by thee, thou shalt not be to him as an usurer, neither shalt thou lay upon him usury.

Proverbs 19:17

He that hath pity upon the poor lendeth unto the LORD; and that which he hath given will he pay him again.

Proverbs 11:15

He that is surety for a stranger shall smart for it: and he that hateth suretiship is sure.

Proverbs 17:18

A man void of understanding striketh hands, and becometh surety in the presence of his friend.

Luke 6:35

Give, and it shall be given unto you; good measure, pressed down, and shaken together, and running over, shall men give into your bosom. For with the same measure that ye mete withal it shall be measured to you again.

Luke 14:28

For which of you, intending to build a tower, sitteth not down first, and counteth the cost, whether he have sufficient to finish it?

Psalm 24:1
The earth is the Lord's and the fullness thereof, the world, and those that dwell therein

Psalm 37:26
He is ever merciful, and lendeth; and his seed is blessed.

Luke 6:38
Give, and it shall be given unto you; good measure, pressed down, and shaken together, and running over, shall men give into your bosom. For with the same measure that ye mete withal it shall be measured to you again.

II Corinthians 9:6
But this I say, He which soweth sparingly shall reap also sparingly; and he which soweth bountifully shall reap also bountifully.

II Corinthians 9:8-9
And God is able to make all grace abound toward you; that ye, always having all sufficiency in all things, may abound to every good work: (As it is written, He hath dispersed abroad; he hath given to the poor: his righteousness remaineth for ever.

Ecclesiastes 5:13-16
There is a sore evil which I have seen under the sun, namely, riches kept for the owners thereof to their hurt. But those riches perish by evil travail: and he begetteth a son, and there is nothing in his hand. As he came forth of his mother's womb, naked shall he return to go as he came, and shall take nothing of his labour, which he may carry away in his hand. And this also is a sore evil, that in all points as he came, so shall he go: and what profit hath he that hath laboured for the wind?

I Timothy 6:17-19

Charge them that are rich in this world, that they be not highminded, nor trust in uncertain riches, but in the living God, who giveth us richly all things to enjoy; That they do good, that they be rich in good works, ready to distribute, willing to communicate; Laying up in store for themselves a good foundation against the time to come, that they may lay hold on eternal life.

Haggai 1:6-7

Ye have sown much, and bring in little; ye eat, but ye have not enough; ye drink, but ye are not filled with drink; ye clothe you, but there is none warm; and he that earneth wages earneth wages to put it into a bag with holes. Thus saith the LORD of hosts; Consider your ways.

Notes

For information on other publications, or to arrange
bookings for workshops and seminars, please contact:

Brian S. Hankerson, CPA
Hankerson and Associates, LLC
341 N 66th Terrace
Hollywood, FL 33024
(954) 295-1954

brianhcpa@aol.com
www.globalministriesint.org